I0162864

Reflections: *Yesterday, Today, Tomorrow*
An Essay on Living

By Marcus H England

Living: Reflections

Scripture quotations were taken predominately from the King James Version of the Bible.

For Information please contact:
Marcus H England at mhe83@aol.com

Inside

Preface

Living is a not a right. Living is not a science. Living is a God – given privilege. God has given each of us the opportunity to experience what life brings. Are we taking full advantage of this opportunity? Throughout my life, I have experienced a myriad of thoughts, gone through trials, and witnessed things that have influenced how I live my life. Whether you are black, red, brown, Asian, or white, "living" brings about a lot similarities. Our lives may be different, but living establishes a level of "sameness"- things we all share i.e., circumstances, problems, successes, beliefs and thoughts. Naturally, I have opinions and thoughts on what living means. In this essay, I share my thoughts and opinions on several subject areas that have affected my life in no small way.

Either you live or you do not. Living is an action verb and thus, requires action. We set the tone. I am certainly not an expert on the subject of Living but I have a point of view that may resonate with most people. On a personal level, living includes four key elements: ***persistence, esteem, courage, and faith.*** These elements have punctuated my life in a very positive way. Throughout these pages, these elements will come to the surface as I talk about my life experiences and thoughts on various topics. Forgive me in advance, if I come across as some type of "pundit". Although my opinions and thoughts are somewhat subjective or even empirical in nature, I hope that you will find enough commonality with them so that you are encouraged you to turn your life around or to continue your current best practices of being the best that you can be.

Without any doubt, God is at the center of my life. That was not always the case. However, make no mistake - God has always been in my life – just not in the center. For many years, I took many things for granted- as so many people do. It took maturity and a full acceptance on my part to fully understand that God is the reason that I exist and that while I am here, I should *live* to please Him. There are [those] times when I struggle at living – but who doesn't? However, I have a foundation that is superior to all and that does not "give way" when I lean heavily upon it! I have absolutely no doubt that I am being led to write this essay at this particular time in my life.

When I am old and gray headed, O God, do not forsake me, until I declare Your strength to this generation. **- Psalm 71:18**

I am a huge proponent of giving back. Psalm 71:18 reminds us of the value of a life well lived and of the worth of lessons learned. Lessons are not just for our benefit. They are meant to be passed along to the next generations. As we all go through our life journey, we should be cognizant of our legacy – perceived or otherwise. I truly believe that "giving back" will be my legacy.

Living: Reflections

Living is not an easy task and I certainly have not mastered it. However, I have lived long enough to have witnessed a tremendous amount of what life can and cannot bring. Beware of those "perfect people" who seemingly on the outside, have it all! No one is immune to imperfection or issues – great or small. Living is a journey of growth and we never cease growing. We are all different but we are also all the same. Through considerable self-esteem development, persistence, courage, and faith, I have overcome many, many obstacles. There may be many of you who may have lost all hope, desire, trust, or even the will to live -for whatever reason. I implore you not to give up! You DO have a purpose in life. I strongly believe that we cannot control life, but we can control living. Have the faith that you can do it. Have the courage to do it. Have the persistence to do it. Develop your esteem. Living.

I hope you enjoy the essay!

Acknowledgements

Writing this essay would not be possible without the infinite presence of God in my life. To Him I give praise and thanks, unabashedly. To my soul mate and wife Jacqueline, thanks for your un-denied love for me through thick and thin. To my two adult children, Candice and Marcus, thanks for being independent and interdependent of each other. I love each of you without condition. To my parents, thanks for "raising me right" and instilling the principles of a good work ethic, independence, and Christianity into my life. To my brothers, and only sister, thanks for family and understanding. To the many friends and acquaintances that I have made over the years, I appreciate and value our relationships. Be encouraged.

One

In the Beginning...

I was born into this world in Norfolk, Virginia on a Tuesday evening in April 1961. I was a healthy 10-pound (big head) boy. According to my mother, I was a very difficult birth. I caused my mother tremendous physical pain and turbulence during childbirth. Although she acknowledges that all of her pregnancies were difficult, mine was singled out as her very worst. Despite that, my mother endured. She even had one more child after me! Today, she will tell anyone who will listen that I was a momma's boy - and I am in total agreement with her.

While an infant, I became very sick with pneumonia and I almost did not make it. My mother reminds me of this from time to time. I had a very high fever and the doctors and nurses knew of only one way to reduce it. They filled a tub with ice and water and soaked me in it in order to bring my fever down. My mother thought they were going to kill me rather than save me! My mother said that I was so cold, I turned blue. However, the doctors and nurses were persistent and soaked me in that tub of ice and water until the fever broke. During that moment as an infant, and going through such a trial, I persevered and survived. However, I realize now that through it all, I was not alone. God was with me and for me. It was obvious that I was meant to be a survivor. It was God's will for me to be here today. For that, I am extremely grateful. Even with all of the trials, tribulations, disappointments, and shortcomings, that would be in my future, I am still grateful that I survived because I have a story to tell.

Two

Dad and Mom

"Honor your father and your mother, so that you may live long in the land the LORD *your God is giving you". Exodus 20:12*

My dad's name was Paul. He passed away in November 2005. He was what I like to refer to as a "man's man". First, he was *all* man. Although dad was small in stature (5'7, 150 lbs.) he was physically very strong. Dad was also handsome and had "the gift of gab" (something I do not have). He appreciated men being men. He could relate [to] and communicate easily and effortless with any man regardless of their perceived stature in life – great or small. Secondly, he had a genuine concern for people that really permeated through his actions. He was

9

extremely generous to a fault. Dad had a very good reputation in the community and was well liked by everyone– especially by senior citizens whom he respected greatly (perhaps he is the reason that I have the utmost respect for senior citizens). Oh, and the ladies liked dad too - much to the disdainment of my mom. Unless they were family, she did not appreciate it too much.

For even when we were with you, we would give you this command: If anyone is not willing to work, let him not eat. - **2 Thessalonians 3:10**

My dad was not afraid of work. He served in the Army and was employed by the federal government. Back in the day, a government job was considered a "lucrative" job to have. Dad retired from the federal government after 35 years of service, but got another job and worked another fifteen years (which help put me through college) and then "retired" again. My dad was the breadwinner and provider (my mom did not have a job, but she was the Chief Financial Officer and Chief Executive Officer)! Dad was the opposite of lazy. He was always busy working on something around the house – "fixing" things. Dad was also a backyard mechanic. As a young boy, I was very impressed with my dad and admired his inclination to go off to work every day and then come home and work. It was extremely rare for him to quit or give up on a project. I possess that "no quit" trait today.

Persistence prevails when all else fails. **-Unknown**

My dad's schooling was limited to the 3rd grade. He had to quit school and work to help his family. Times were difficult in the 1930s and work was more important than school for most families. If you were lucky, you went to school. My dad was an unlucky one. Those were the options from which families had to choose –school or work. Perhaps that is why my dad put so much value on education for his children. He absolutely valued education – something he was denied. However, even with the lack of a "formal" education, I considered my dad very astute and very wise. Frankly, his level of knowledge and wisdom on a plethora of subjects amazed me at times.

Dad became a born again Christian "later in life" – when I was a teenager. Even before that transformation, he was a loving, kind, and generous of his time and resources. However, he realized that he was missing something bigger in his life and decided to give his life to Christ. After giving his life to Christ, he became an even better person. He was totally committed to pleasing God and he taught as many people as he could touch, the virtues of Christian living. The Lord led dad to teach and spread the Word and dad was obedient (not unlike another Paul). Dad was also a good steward. It took a great deal of courage for dad to "leave" his drinking buddies and follow Jesus. Nevertheless, he did it with no regrets. He quickly became well respected in church and in "church circles" for his biblical acumen and teaching ability, his humility, his desire to serve, and his steadfastness. Dad had an impact on the lives of many people. He was a natural leader and people loved to follow him because of his integrity and common sense (more on common sense later). He became a student of the bible and could quote and memorize scripture like no one I have ever known. He "schooled" many a preacher on things that you would think they would know. Dad also walked the walk- yet remained full of humility, compassion, and generosity. Was dad perfect? Absolutely not. Nevertheless, he was a perfect example to me in many ways.

His lord said unto him, Well done, thou good and faithful servant: thou hast been faithful over a few things, I will make thee ruler over many things: enter thou into the joy of thy lord. **- Matthew 25:21**

In November 2005, after battling emphysema for several years, my dad went home to Glory. He was 82 years old. I helped eulogize my father and spoke on the topic "A Good Example". He was a very good example to me and to many, many others as well. I have no doubt that the Lord received dad into his Kingdom immediately. Dad's faith was immense and unwavering to the very end. Even on his deathbed, he was concerned for others and their salvation. He showed me how to live and he showed me how to die.

I am not my dad, nor will I ever be. It is natural for a young boy to want to be like his father and I was no different. However, as I matured, I wanted to create my own identity and fate – be my own man. I am glad that I did. My dad understood this and appreciated it too. All of us are individuals with life templates made up of different algorithms. I have put it upon myself to live in such a manner such that I will see my dad again in the Kingdom. I miss my dad, but I am comforted by his memory. The legacy he left behind permeates throughout my life. He did not just exist, he lived. For that, I honor him, even now.

My mom's name is Ruth. She is in her mid eighties now and still resides in the same house that I grew up in. My mom was what they refer to now as a "stay at home mom". As I mentioned earlier, she was the CFO and CEO. Without mom, our household would not have run very efficiently. She did the budgeting, shopping, cooking, laundry, "made market", and paid the bills. Mom took care of the home – period. She worked. When she worked, you worked too! You did not lie in the bed all day in her house. That thought never crossed your mind! As a child growing up, my mom was the focal point for me. I was not the youngest, but I was still a momma's boy. I just felt a certain closeness to her (and to her mom, my grandmother too). She was both disciplinarian and comforter. My dad lovingly nicknamed her "Heavy" – not because of her size (mom was not a large woman) but because she was the heavy hitter! Mom is actually a quiet person but strong-willed. She will not hesitate to let you know what is on her mind.

Living: Reflections

From an early age, my mother instilled religion in me. I will forever give credit to her for ensuring that I went to church EVERY Sunday and encouraging me to be an active member as well. It was an unspoken rule – if it's Sunday and you reside in her house, you went to church. My mom ensured that Jesus was a big part of my life. My faith in Jesus was obtained at an early age. I acted in church Christmas plays (these plays were grand productions and I was a top actor), read scripture (from the sacred grounds of the pulpit), and was active in Sunday school (I taught a Sunday school class as a teenager). I even served as "youth preacher" once and gave a sermon (the sermon topic escapes me). Most of the "old church ladies" thought that I would grow up and be a preacher. They would say "boy, you goin be a preacha". They were absolutely and positively certain that I would become a preacher when I grew up. I often think about their "prophesy".

Living: Reflections

As I mentioned earlier, I was a momma's boy. If you said something negative about my mom, those were fighting words. Really. I took offense to any negativity or mocking in reference to her. My mom was somewhat "protective" of me too. For example, she would never sign my permission slips allowing me to play sports! She said that she did not want me to get hurt so I had to ask dad to sign. Although this was problematic, she could care less about sports.

Perhaps out of sincere gratitude and respect, I never called my dad and mom by their first names – no matter how old I was. I never considered them my friends either. They are my parents-period. That is just a personal thing with me. They are the only dad and mom that I can ever have. Dad and mom were married for 59 years. Although dad passed away five years ago, she still misses him. She is in reasonably good health and is very independent- still likes to shop, still cooks, still drives (Lexus), and is still the heavy hitter! I call her at least three times a week and try to visit her once a month. Without her prayers, I know that I would be in a different place today. I am absolutely sure of that. There is nothing like the prayers of a mother. For me, every day is mother's day. I am grateful to God that my mom is still around. To say that my mom has been a very good mother is an understatement. Was she tough? Yes. Did I not like her at times as a child because of her discipline? Absolutely. However, in the total scheme of things, I would not trade her for any other. I appreciate the fashion in which she raised me. Dad found a good woman in my mother. The good Lord kept them together for 59 years for a reason. Living.

Who can find a virtuous woman? for her price is far above rubies. The heart of her husband doth safely trust in her, so that he shall have no need of spoil. She will do him good and not evil all the days of her life. She seeketh wool, and flax, and worketh willingly with her hands. She is like the merchants' ships; she bringeth her food from afar. She riseth also while it is yet night, and giveth meat to her household and a portion to her maidens. She considereth a field, and buyeth it: with the fruit of her hands she planteth a vineyard. ¹⁷ She girdeth her loins with strength, and *strengtheneth her arms. She perceiveth that her merchandise is good: her candle goeth not out by night. She layeth her hands to the spindle, and her hands hold the distaff. She stretcheth out her hand to the poor; yea, she reacheth forth her hands to the needy. She is not afraid of the snow for her household: for all her household are clothed with scarlet. She maketh herself coverings of tapestry; her clothing is silk and purple. Her husband is known in the gates, when he sitteth among the elders of the land. She maketh fine linen, and selleth it; and delivereth girdles unto the merchant. Strength and honour are her clothing; and she shall rejoice in time to come. She openeth her mouth with wisdom; and in her tongue is the law of kindness. She looketh well to the ways of her household, and eateth not the bread of idleness. Her children arise up, and call her blessed; her husband also, and he praiseth her. Many daughters have done virtuously, but thou excellest them all. Favour is deceitful, and beauty is vain: but a woman that feareth the LORD, she shall be praised. Give her of the fruit of her hands; and let her own works praise her in the gates.* **- *Proverbs 31: 11-31***

Three

The Uncertainty of Life

There is one thing certain about life, its uncertainty. Why? Life on earth is not meant to be perfect. When you wake up each day, you have no "realistic" idea what will happen with you. Do not presume that you know God's Will. You cannot possibly know what is going to happen from one moment to the next. However, you must plan as if you do know. You cannot control life, but you can control living.

Now listen, you who say, "Today or tomorrow we will go to this or that city, spend a year there, carry on business and make money." Why, you do not even know what will happen tomorrow. What is your life? You are a mist that appears for a little while and then vanishes. **- James 4:13-14**

Take one day at a time. Life is exactly what you make of it. This is a very common challenge that is given to those people who are in a hurry. Indeed, it is sound advice. Trusting in God to lead your steps is also sound advice.

Trust in God with all your heart and lean not unto your own understanding. In all thy ways acknowledge Him and He will direct your path. **- Proverbs 3:5-6.**

Taking one day at a time and trusting in God to lead your steps provide you with a sense of direction and assurance. One thing that I have learned over the years is that life is full of "surprises". There are times when you are presented with unexpected events that really knock you off stride. How do you respond - is the key to dealing with life's "trials". Will you over react? Under react? Or just complain – why me? It is very easy to display self-pity when things do not go our way.

"If I had a formula for bypassing trouble, I wouldn't pass it around. I wouldn't be doing anyone a favor. Trouble creates a capacity to handle it . . . . Meet it as a friend, for you'll see a lot of it and you had better be on speaking terms with it." **- Oliver Wendell Holmes**

I recommend taking the focus off you and focus on being better prepared. How do you prepare for the unexpected? First, equip yourself with the power of God's "covering" through prayer. God is always available to guide you through life's unexpected journey. Have faith that He will lead you through. Second, you must accept the fact that adversity will occur. As long as we live, we will go through some adversity. Put yourself in the right frame of mind that will allow you to have confidence and accept life's unexpected "plums" and view them as challenges. The apostle Paul unexpectedly had a thorn in his flesh. Paul certainly did not see this coming. Although he prayed to have it removed, it was not! Even with the thorn, Paul drew nigh to God and continued preaching the Gospel of Jesus Christ despite persecutions and imprisonment.

So teach us to number our days, that we may apply our hearts unto wisdom. **- Psalms 90:12**

Living: Reflections

Life is akin to a flickering flame. Our days are numbered from before birth. Therefore, we should treat our lives as the fragile properties of the Creator that they are. We are but temporary stewards [here] on earth. Therefore, what we do while we are here is extremely important. Although our earthly life is full of uncertainty, our eternal life is as promised – full of peace and fellowship, free of suffering, free of sin, and perfect with the Lord forever.

 So prepare yourself for the uncertainty of life on earth by asking God for covering and the courage to face the challenges that await you. Have faith that you will overcome them. It took me many years to adopt this mindset. Nevertheless, I am glad that I finally did. I am living proof that God will deliver you through a multitude of situations and I am a better person for it. You will be better as well. Living.

Four

Playing Ball

Sports saved my life – literally. I was an extremely quiet child. I was quieter than a church mouse in the pulpit! When I had something to say, I did not say it. I was very shy too. It was a struggle to be out front and my self-esteem was non-existent. I kept all thoughts and feelings inside. Besides, I could never understand why people talked so much anyway (and I still do not)! There were entire days when I would not say a single word. However, my mind was always constantly at work – churning. I truly believe that my family thought something was wrong with me. Something was. I was extremely sad and lonely. I was depressed. My life was a melancholy existence. There were days when I would think about ways to end my life. I did not think anyone understood me. There was a tremendous internal struggle taking place. My friends and family had no idea how I felt. I was a genius at hiding my emotions. I was very quiet but my mind was very noisy.

I honestly believe that it was because of my low self-esteem that I gravitated toward sports. I felt the need to be included and to contribute in such a way that was appreciated. Sports allowed both of those things. Playing sports required a certain amount of discipline, unselfishness, passion, and determination. Playing sports gives you a sense of accomplishment because not everybody can "play". To play sports meant that you belonged to an exclusive club – again, everybody could not play sports and "make the team".

I was a slender child – six o'clock on stilts. So initially, I was extremely self-conscious about my physique or lack thereof. The rest of my friends all seemed to be stronger and had muscles everywhere. Most country boys are naturally strong anyway – and I *was* strong, but I was all legs and arms! Nevertheless, I felt so strongly about belonging, I tried every sport available – baseball, softball, basketball, football, even ping-pong (I was ping-pong champ of my neighborhood for a few summers)! I needed an escape from the gloominess of my life. In the beginning, I was not great at any of them. I wasn't very athletic so I had to work harder than most of my peers. Sports provided me with the opportunity to demonstrate a work ethic that my dad possessed.

Although I already had a certain amount of determination before I began playing sports, sports allowed me to showcase and demonstrate it. I practiced harder and outworked my teammates. I took pride in that. At age 12, I also began lifting weights (cement filled plastic weights) because I was being teased about being so skinny. I was a laughing stock of the neighborhood. Some of my "friends" were just plain brutal with their teasing. However, I kept lifting and lifting and coming back. The teasing actually motivated me to work even harder.

Before long, my body began to reflect the weightlifting and the hundreds of daily pushups that made up my "workout regimen". I still wasn't very athletic, but at least my body was becoming muscular! As I mentioned before, I was naturally strong but then I became very strong. This really helped my self-esteem and gave me confidence not just in reference to sports but confidence in other areas. I wasn't as self-conscious about my body. When I walked into a room, I walked in "tall" and with a purpose – but I was still somewhat shy.

I played baseball, softball, basketball, and football up until the seventh grade. After that, it was football, basketball, and track. I was becoming a better athlete – still not athletic like my friends – but I overachieved by out-working them. I became a competitor, but I was not a sore loser. Basketball was my favorite sport but I was not good enough to thrive and make the school team (cut from Junior High team). Therefore, by the ninth grade, I decided that football would be the sport for me. Football is a very physical sport. For some reason, I loved the physical contact. It was very challenging to hit someone yet keep yourself healthy.

I played Junior High, JV and Varsity football - moving up the ranks each year with hard work and determination. The odds of me making and "starting" for my varsity team one day seemed only remote a few years earlier. The high school football program that I would enter had a very rich and successful history. However, I was determined to make the first team AND to get a football scholarship if only to prove to my "friends" and myself that I was good enough. I earned first team varsity midway through my junior year and did not relinquish it. I had a very good senior season and our team was one win from making the playoffs.

After my senior year, I received interest from a few small schools in Virginia and North Carolina. Only a few people knew that I had played my entire senior season with a partially torn groin. It was painful beyond measure. But my threshold for pain is extremely high and I persevered. Who would have guessed that I would be good enough to receive a full football scholarship? In 1979, I received and I accepted a full football scholarship from a small CIAA school in southwestern Virginia. However, because my severe groin injury had not completely healed, I never played a single down. Although I was disappointed, I won! I had achieved my goal of earning a college football scholarship.

Playing competitive sports was over. Through the subsequent years, I truly missed playing football and suffered with a great deal of regret (as hindsight usually brings) along with the "what ifs". Football taught me lessons of discipline, mental toughness, teamwork, willpower, communication, and dealing with adversity- all life lessons. These were lessons learned that would benefit me greatly through the years. Playing sports was definitely a critical turning point in my life. It served as a validation of sorts - I could be successful against the highest of odds. It grasped me from the depths of low self-esteem, loneliness, and doubt. Hard work, persistence, and determination were all attributes and keys to my success while playing football.

Needless to say, these attributes and keys are a large part of my life today that has allowed me to get through certain doors that I otherwise would not have been able to get through. It was truly serendipitous. I was only looking for an escape from sadness and acceptance! Because of my experiences of playing sports, I became a huge advocate of youth sports. I coached youth basketball and served as a certified basketball official for many years.

I highly encourage young people to put down their electronic devices and give sports a try. You may not make the team, but the payoff of trying to make the team can be very beneficial. If it had not been for sports, I honestly don't know where I would be today. Sports were truly my saving grace. Living.

Five

Patience and Prayer

Knowing this, that the trying of your faith worketh patience. But let patience have her perfect work, that ye may be perfect and entire, wanting nothing. **- James 1: 3-4**

Oh, the patience of Job! Good things happen to those who wait. What happened to Job is worth visiting. Satan caused severe troubles for Job when God permitted him to suffer under Satan's hand. However, Job was steadfast in his faith – even when his "friends" tried to persuade him that *he* was the cause of his own great suffering and loss! Nevertheless, Job was patient and prayed to God with humility and insight.

Living: Reflections

Naked came I out of my mother's womb, and naked shall I return thither: the LORD gave, and the LORD hath taken away; blessed be the name of the LORD. **- Job 1:20-22**

Patience is probably the most difficult of virtues. We are living in times where instant gratification abounds but Job's patience is unsurpassed. However, we should all strive toward Job's level of patience. Are you a patient person? I have grown to become more patient over the years in many areas but there is plenty of room for improvement. Personally, it has been a journey that has required maturation in the right areas. Thus, I can still be rather impatient in certain areas. For example, I do not have much patience for foolishness. I view foolishness as a personal choice. This is different from being ignorant, which I define as someone who just does not know any better. Think of foolishness as being someone being intentionally ignorant.

According to the bible, we are to pray unceasingly

(1 Thessalonians 5: 17). We should pray at all times and make prayer a part of our daily lives. Regardless of what you may be doing, or where you are, you can still pray. By the way, there is nothing fancy about prayer. Prayer is simply a personal conversation with God. I often hear long drawn out "fanciful" prayers and I cringe. You do not receive any style points for these types of "shows".

But when ye pray, use not vain repetitions, as the heathen do: for they think that they shall be heard for their much speaking. **- Matthew 6:7**

Our God knows what we need before we even ask! Therefore, get to the point and get there quickly! God wants us to pray. When we pray, it pleases Him. Why? Because when we pray, we are first conceding that we believe in God and second, that we trust Him to answer. Belief, confidence, and trust – these should be the "core" components of all prayers. All of these components require patience.

The bible exhorts us to pray for others because God wants all people to be saved.

I exhort therefore, that, first of all, supplications, prayers, intercessions, and giving of thanks, be made for all men. **- Timothy 2:1-5**

My mother's prayers have sustained me throughout the years. She prays fervently for her children every day. I encourage you to intercede for others through prayer. Prayer is uplifting and can serve as a covering of assurance and well-being. But remember, God answers your prayer according to His time. It was not until Job prayed for his "friends" that God restored him and made him prosperous again.

For sure, it can be difficult to be patient at times. As they say some people, things, or situations can really "try your patience". But with continued effort and faith, you can improve your patience capacity and reduce your stress to boot! Pray for patience and "wait on the Lord". Just remember, God may not come when you want Him to, but He is always right on time.

Patience and prayer are interdependent and intertwined. We all must go through trials and when we do, our patience is really put to the test. Read the Book of Job. It will give you strength, encouragement, guidance, and a lesson in patience and prayer. Be patient. Be prayerful. Living.

After Job had prayed for his friends, the LORD made him prosperous again and gave him twice as much as he had before. **- Job 42:10**

Living: Reflections

Six

Common Sense

If common sense was so common, why don't more people have it? This is not a rhetorical question! I do not consider myself very smart- but I do consider myself to have common sense. It is an important enough topic that I could not ignore it when it came to writing this essay. Common sense is an essential part of my life. The lack of common sense is no laughing matter. The lack of common sense can cause some very serious problems. But [just] what is common sense? Common sense is a rare quality that people have. I define it as the ability to utilize good practical judgment in situations that demand good practical judgment. I do not believe that common sense can be taught nor is it a learned trade. It is inherent with one's birth- at least that's my firm belief. It is the sixth sense. Either you have common sense or you do not. It is that simple.

Over the years, I have seen some of the most absurd actions, reactions, and decisions that anyone would ever want to see. Professionals and government leaders, clergy, and "academic scholars", etc. who make befuddling, and outright stupid comments and do wonderfully peculiar things. It just goes to show you that common sense is as evasive as perfection is! This "phenomenon" (lack of common sense) infiltrates many people no matter their walk in life. Clap your hands if you know people who have no common sense!

Just like everything else in life, striking a balance works best. Some people actually have too much common sense! Having too much common sense is just as problematic as having no common sense at all. I do not believe that you should flaunt your common sense (although my wife may testify that I "flaunt" mine sometimes). Having too much common sense is certainly not innocuous by any means. There are people who are constantly "thinking" up ways to be one-step ahead but end up out-thinking themselves. The problem is that they usually end up making the situation more complicated that it needs to be. Unknowingly, they get in their own way and therefore are their own worst enemy. Clap your hands if you know someone who has too much common sense!

It is a thousand times better to have common sense without education than to have education without common sense.
- *Robert G. Ingersoll*

As I stated earlier, I do not consider myself very smart. In fact, if it were not for common sense, I would not have made it through college. There were just enough courses that required common sense (versus courses that demanded book sense) that enabled me to get through (I actually graduated with a degree in Business Administration in three years). Thank God my professional career has also panned out this way. Most of my jobs have required more common sense aptitude than theory or other technical practicalities. As I analyze work related problems or perform data analysis, I use a common sense approach – and I must say, I have been successful – for the most part.

One of my favorite people in history is former U. S. Supreme Court Justice, Thurgood Marshall -the first black to serve on the Supreme Court. Although I did not know a whole lot about his personal history, I do know that he was a pillar in the black community during segregation that stood up for the rights of the poor. He was a courageous man and a strong advocate and lawyer for civil rights long before he became our nations' first black Solicitor General and then the first black member of our nation's highest court. However, even with all that he stood and fought for, Thurgood Marshall, as a Supreme Court Justice was famous for his common sense and clarity. He wrote important majority opinions in Bounds v. Smith (1977), which defended prisoners' rights to legal assistance and libraries, and Stanley v. Georgia (1969), which protected the rights of individuals to possess pornography. His opinion in the Stanley case illustrates the common sense and clarity for which he was famous:

"If the First Amendment means anything, it means that the state has no business telling a man, sitting alone in his own house, what books he may read or what films he may watch."

Of course, conservatives had their qualms about Thurgood Marshall, but even they respected his plainspoken, common sense approach. When he retired from the court at age 83, an interviewer asked how he wished to be remembered. He was characteristically plainspoken and blunt, saying, "He did the best he could with what he had." I remember watching that interview and being so impressed by that answer from a person of his stature and I acquiesced. From a man who did so much for so many and who served on the highest court of the land, that was a common sense answer if ever there was one. Thank God for common sense. Living.

Seven

(Hello) Friend

"The most important ingredient we put into any relationship is not what we say or what we do, but what we are. And if our words and our actions come from superficial human relations techniques (the Personality Ethic) rather than from our own inner core (the Character Ethic), others will sense that duplicity. We simply won't be able to create and sustain the foundation necessary for effective interdependence."

- Stephen R. Covey

Relationships are a vital and substantive part of everyday living. Friends and families are the centerpiece of many of our lives. Nevertheless, no relationship is perfect and without blemish. With relationships come the inevitable strains and disappointments. Someone will invariably let another person down. Someone will allow selfishness to intervene. Someone will slay you with his or her tongue. Someone will fail to forgive. Someone's "true character" will peek through unexpectedly. That is the nature of relationships. Everyone who claims to be your friend may not be your friend.

When I was growing up, I had many friends. I even had a best friend. We played together, fought each other, and played together again! We would fight for each other too. As years passed by, I intentionally begin to scale down the size of my "friend network". I found that friends are mostly fair weather and I often lacked commonality with most of them anyway. In other words, I realized that I did not need to have friends for the sake of having friends. The term "friend" is extremely loose. Many of my friends have disappointed me (false friends will betray you) and I found myself being a little judgmental too. Being judgmental is not what friends do to each other. Today, I choose to have mostly "acquaintances" instead (I still have friends). In fact, I have many acquaintances – some closer than others.

My definition of an acquaintance is someone that I am comfortable being around when I see them; they are supportive, reliable, and dependable. Yet, we can go our separate ways without emotional distress and be okay. I do not need to see them nor do I need to speak with them regularly in order to maintain our "relationship". A friend is closer and is someone with whom you are emotionally attached [to]. A friend is someone you can wholly trust. That is a big deal. I have a few friends, and my wife is one of them. I do not believe that I could live without friends. My acquaintances would probably consider me their friend, and I am fine with that. Let it be known that acquaintances can become friends in a heartbeat! Because I have more acquaintances than friends, I have the necessary relationships that make living "livable" minus the drama. I would have it no other way.

Living: Reflections

Relationships are essential to living. No one should think that they are alone in this world without love, care, and support. It is just as important to be a friend or even an acquaintance. We all need one another to make each other stronger as we make our journey through life. Love to live. Live to love someone. We *are* our brother's keeper. Living.

Eight

I Wonder

Have you wondered what heaven is like? Sometimes I wonder. It's funny because as I grow older, I have begun to think more and more about heaven (I don't think about hell- as I don't plan to go there)! So, what will heaven be like? When loved ones, family, and friends pass away, we often say, "They are in a better place now and at peace". We are saying that because the assumption is that they went to heaven and not hell. But what does "at peace" mean?

The bible depicts heaven as a "real place":

Revelation 22 says " Then the angel showed me the river of the water of life, as clear as crystal, flowing from the throne of God and of the Lamb down the middle of the great street of the city. On each side of the river stood the tree of life, bearing twelve crops of fruit, yielding its fruit every month. And the leaves of the tree are for the healing of the nations. No longer will there be any curse. The throne of God and of the Lamb will be in the city, and his servants will serve him. They will see his face, and his name will be on their foreheads. There will be no more night. They will not need the light of a lamp or the light of the sun, for the Lord God will give them light. And they will reign forever and ever. The angel said to me, "These words are trustworthy and true. The Lord, the God of the spirits of the prophets, sent his angel to show his servants the things that must soon take place."

Heaven will include all races, nationalities, sexes, and skin colors. Whom will I see? Who will I recognize? What will people look like? What type of food will be available? What will a typical day be like? How's the weather? How big is heaven? For sure, Moses, Paul, Enoch, Job, Peter, John, Noah, Isaiah, Stephen and other biblical stalwarts will be there. Will I be able to talk to them? Will I be surprised by who made it in and who did not? These are just some of the thoughts that have crossed my mind but not in a perfunctory manner. I guess that I shouldn't worry about what heaven is like and just be satisfied that it exists and that it is promised to everyone who believes that Jesus died for our sins, was raised from the dead, and is alive today serving as our intercessor to the Throne of God. However, wondering about heaven gives me motivation to try my very best to get there.

There are people who have passed away that I want to see again - such as my loved ones. Although I often wonder about heaven, I can live with knowing that it will be just as the bible describes it. My task now is to live in such a manner that on That Day, at the Appointed Time, I will be welcomed into heaven- never, ever to leave. Still, I wonder. Living.

Living: Reflections

Nine

Wash Your Mouth!

I am not ashamed to say that I have never been one to have a "vulgar" tongue. I have been guilty of many things in my life, but having a "colorful" mouth is not one of them. I do not know what it is about cursing or cussing (they may be different and I will use the terms profanity, cursing, and cussing, interchangeably here) but I have never been an advocate. Back in the day, only grown folks cursed; children did not. Today, everybody does, including church folk. In fact, many a church folk will "bless you real good"! You hear profanity at the movies, in music videos, at the office, in restaurants, and in parks. In other words, you hear profanity in everyday conversations. It's everywhere. I would not be surprised if there was somebody in a church, somewhere cussing somebody out -

right now! Now let me confess, from time to time, a "choice word" does escape from me. However, it is very rare that it does. When I say "vulgar mouth", I mean those persons whose "normal" everyday vocabulary is full of profanity-spilled musings.

I think for some people, cursing is as normal as riding a bike. Children grow up hearing their parents, family members, and friends using curse words regularly and in turn, they pass it on to their children. In fact, the "cussing gene" is passed on from generation to generation. For some, when they first began to curse, it's akin to a rite of passage – I'm old enough to curse now!

My parents did not use profanity. However, from time to time, my mom would "let the S-Word slip" but that was extremely rare. She had to be very upset with you for that to happen. As for my father, I never heard him say a single curse word – at least not in front of me.

Some people just cannot help but to use profanity. It is the only way for them to "effectively" communicate in order to make a point. It matters not where they are or the circumstance. They will curse and cuss and cuss and curse without hesitation or shame. They don't have to necessarily be upset with anything or anyone either.

Some people make their living by cursing. Richard Pryor, Chris Rock, Redd Foxx and other comedians get paid to make people laugh and they do it with plenty of cursing. If you've ever heard their standup routines, they will curse as if cursing is going out of style – all in the name of comedy and storytelling. Is all of that profanity really necessary? The comedians that I identified are the best of their prospective generations (Pryor is probably the best ever). In my opinion, they are all naturally funny. They don't need profanity in their routines in order to make people laugh (Bill Cosby, anyone?). However, I guarantee you that if they did not curse in their routines, they would not be as popular. That is just the way it is — seems as though profanity laced tirades are the attraction for comedy seeking fans.

With the tongue we praise our Lord and Father, and with it we curse men, who have been made in God's likeness. Out of the same mouth come praise and cursing. My brothers, this should not be. Can both fresh water and salt water flow from the same spring? My brothers, can a fig tree bear olives, or a grapevine bear figs? Neither can a salt spring produce fresh water.

- James 3:9-12 NIV

I grew up believing that profanity was disrespectful. I still believe this. I also believe that you can stop cursing – if you really want to stop. Cursing is not an addiction, it's a chosen lifestyle (don't get me wrong; cursing doesn't make you a bad person and not cursing doesn't make you a good person) it's just my belief that it's unnecessary. Therefore, there is hope that you can clean up your vocabulary. Wash your mouth! Living.

Living: Reflections

Ten

Maintenance

Are you in shape? Obviously, good health is very important. However, a lot of us take our health for granted or think we can wait before we get ourselves together (men in particular). We should all take care of our bodies. I must admit that my diet is extremely poor. I eat anything – red meat, pork (I love bacon), and all manner of seafood. If it tastes good, I will eat it. As a country boy, I grew up eating what my mother cooked. For sure, it wasn't the healthiest of foods and I certainly can't blame her for my poor diet. Nevertheless, today, I am paying for my bad eating habits. I have high blood pressure (although it may be hereditary) and high cholesterol. I take medication for both and they are "under control".

Living: Reflections

A few years ago, I had a "medical scare". During a routine annual physical, (I have a "full physical" every year) my EKG (charts the electrical activity of the heart) was "abnormal" and I was asked to have further testing. A few weeks later, I performed a stress test and my EKG remained abnormal. At that time, I was told that an abnormal EKG reading can be a "normal" reading, however, I was asked to take an echocardiogram (uses sound waves to create visual images of the heart) and I did. After this test, I was asked to take an MRI of the heart and have a cardiac catheterization (dye is pumped into your heart chamber via your wrist or groin to see how your heart muscles are working and if the valves are opening and closing properly) performed. It was at this point that I began to get a little concerned. Did I have a blockage? Did I have a "bad" heart? I prayed for the best results possible but also decided that I had to live with whatever the results were. After taking this third test, I had to wait a week for the results. This was around Christmas time and I was not in a holiday mood.

Living: Reflections

I anxiously awaited the results. After a week, I called to find out the results and to my relief, I was informed that I did not have a blockage and that my heart was functioning properly – my abnormal EKG reading was normal. What a relief! I was again reminded that because of my high blood pressure and high cholesterol, I should avoid salt and high sodium foods. In other words, change my eating habits. I must say that I have improved my diet (although I have a long way to go). I still eat what I want, but in moderation. In other words, I don't eat my favorite foods (bacon, sausage, steak, burgers) every day, I don't use salt at all, and I really watch my sodium intake. I work out at my local gym at least three times a week (though it is difficult to get motivated at times) just to "maintain". Sometimes, it takes a "scare" to get your attention. More than ever, I realize that good health plays a big part in the quality of living.

Do you not know that your body is a temple of the Holy Spirit, who is in you, whom you have received from God? You are not your own; you were bought at a price. Therefore, honor God with your body.

- I Corinthians 6:19-20

It is true that maintaining our bodies is important for good health. It is just as important to maintain a healthy spirit. The spirit is the inner (space) being in all of us having to do with deep (often religious) feelings and beliefs, including a person's sense of peace, purpose, and connection to others. It also includes your beliefs about the meaning of life. Whether it involves meditation, reactivation, or a good scrubbing, we should make sure that our inner being is where it should be. If you don't have a sense of purpose, sense of peace, or a good handle on what life means, then I encourage you to "perform an examination" of your spirit. Give your inner spirit a check-up! Only you can examine your inner being. Your friends and family cannot do it. You must perform a thorough assessment of where you are in life from an inner viewpoint. Frankly, we all get off track, but the good thing is that we can get back on track with effort and determination.

I maintain my spirit by focusing on what is important to me – family, morality, integrity, values, peace, and faith. These are my core beliefs and represent what I want most out of life. They are in my conscious and give me a sense of being and purpose. At times, I have to remind myself of their importance and refocus specifically on how I grade out. Through prayer or intense meditation, I examine my inner being to see if my life is as meaningful as it needs to be and that my goal of going to heaven is still the focus. This is how I "maintain" my inner being.

Finally, brethren, whatever things are true, whatever things are noble, whatever things are just, whatever things are pure, whatever things are lovely, whatever things are of good report, if there is any virtue and if there is anything praiseworthy--meditate on these things. **- Philippians 4:8**

Living: Reflections

Garbage in, garbage out! Regular checkups of our bodies and spirit are highly recommended. They will do your body and spirit good. Are you in shape? Maintain. Living.

Eleven

Time

Time does not care. It has absolutely no feelings or compassion. Yet, time is the most essential element of living. Either you keep up, or you are left behind! To most of us, time can be a myriad of things - unforgiving, relentless, slow, fast, late, to name a few. Truthfully, it is none of those things. Time is a constant - it moves in one direction at the same pace and never changes. Time cannot be stopped or interrupted. Time cannot be touched, heard, seen, tasted, or smelled – but it's all around us. You can reset your clocks all you want [to], time will still be time. It matters not if you have a Rolex or Timex, time will be time. Once it is gone, it's gone forever. In other words, time is always new. Wherever you are, right now is a new time – you have never witnessed it before and you will never witness it again. God created time. He does not use time nor does He need it. He is not bound by it. God is "I am". However, for us, time is the essence of living.

Ben Franklin said it's the stuff that life is made of. We all have the same amount but we all get different results. This is based on how we use it and what we do with it. So this brings up the question we should be asking ourselves - How do I spend my time? To be successful we should be maximizing how we use the minutes of our lives.

I love history. History is simply a time gone by. Although it cannot be "re-lived", it can be a tool in which we can better live our lives. If more people knew their family history, their nation's history, and world history, today's time would be expended more efficiently. Why? There is no better teacher than history! History is full of "mistakes". What better way to value time than to not repeat the mistakes of others who came [in time] before you.

You must learn from the mistakes of others. You can't possibly live long enough to make them all yourself.
- Sam Levenson

Use your time wisely. You have heard this recommendation repeatedly. To most of us, it is easier said than done. It doesn't matter how old you are or your maturity level, using time wisely can be a difficult task. Do you map out your time and corresponding activities? Whether consciously or unconsciously, we all waste a lot of time. We should invest our time in a prudent manner. But why is time so difficult to manage? Have you ever wondered why some people seem to have all the time in the world and you are scrambling around wondering where the time went? They manage time better! They probably view time as an investment commodity. If we all viewed time as the "limited commodity" that it really is, I guarantee you that we would manage it better too. Nevertheless, that is exactly what time is – limited. You have heard the phrase "living on borrowed time". Sure, there are 24 hrs. in a day. However, we have no idea how much of that time we will actually witness because God Himself loans time out to us individually. Time should be treated as an hourglass with fine grains of sand trickling down. We are running out of time and you cannot turn it over and reuse it!

I have a "blurb" that I use from time to time as an ending to letters that I write – "Go Forward". It is a simple point with potentially huge ramifications. As I mentioned, history is a time gone by. My wife does not like to ride the metro rail (while sitting) facing backward. For some reason, it's physically uncomfortable for her. There is another thing about riding in a rail car sitting backward - you see backward! You can only see where you have already been! In other words, you cannot see where you have not been yet. This is what should make you uncomfortable! My blurb "Go Forward" encourages others to see and think forward. It is OK to visit history, just do not stay there! We should all go forward with our ideas, faith, relationships, pursuits, maturation, etc. Going forward transitions process to progress. Are you making progress? By going forward, you don't live in the past nor do you allow past history to define who you are. As difficult as it can be to let go, what's past is past. You cannot re-harvest an onion. Time only goes forward and so should you. This is my time! This is your time! Go Forward! Living.

Twelve

Wisdom

And now, O LORD my God, thou hast made thy servant king instead of David my father: and I am but a little child: I know not how to go out or come in. And thy servant is in the midst of thy people which thou hast chosen, a great people, that cannot be numbered nor counted for multitude. Give therefore thy servant an understanding heart to judge thy people that I may discern between good and bad: for who is able to judge this thy so great a people? And the speech pleased the LORD, that Solomon had asked this thing. And God said unto him, Because thou hast asked this thing, and hast not asked for thyself long life; neither hast asked riches for thyself, nor hast asked the life of thine enemies; but hast asked for thyself understanding to discern judgment; Behold, I have done according to thy words: lo, I have given thee a wise and an understanding heart; so that there was none like thee before thee, neither after thee shall any arise like unto thee. And I have also given thee that which thou hast not asked, both riches, and honour: so that there shall not be any among the kings like unto thee all thy days. **- I Kings 7-13**

God appeared to King Solomon in a dream and tells him "ask for anything you want". Solomon asked for the wisdom to make decisions. God promised him that he would be wiser than any man who had ever lived before him and who will ever live after him. Because Solomon did not ask for long life or riches, God granted both! How many of us would choose wisdom over long life and riches?

As I have matured, obtaining wisdom has become more and more important to me. To me wisdom is having an understanding heart in order to make right and insightful decisions for the greater good. Sounds like a simple concept, but it is not.

One should not confuse being smart or intelligent with wisdom. Wisdom is not about being smart or intelligent. There are people too numerous to count that are smart or intelligent but have no wisdom. Being smart or intelligent typically restricts or limits a person to a certain subject area (although it could include broad subject areas) and the depth of intelligence is limited to one's thinking capacity. In contrast, having wisdom has no limitations and the heart is the key component. The heart allows for a greater depth of discernment of all things through compassion. Your capacity to think is obviously required, but the heart is what differentiates wisdom from mere intelligence.

"As a rule, man's a fool. When it's hot, he wants it cool. And when it's cool, he wants it hot. Always wanting what is not." **- Poet Unknown**

Wisdom should be an integral part of living. I include a provision for wisdom in my daily prayers because I seek to discern as much as possible about understanding how things are supposed to be and why they are supposed to be [that way]. In other words, I seek to increase my compassion for living which in turn will ensure that I make proper decisions. I may never get

73

to the point of being wise, but I plan to continue seeking wisdom through prayer. Living.

Thirteen

50

When I was a child, I spake as a child, I understood as a child, I thought as a child: but when I became a man, I put away childish things.

- I Corinthians 13:11

If it is the will of God, I will be 50 years old in 2011. Although I would have lived more years than I have years yet to live, I will be glad to see it – but not overly glad (as I try to have an even keel about things). Yes, it goes without saying that I will truly be thankful for another year. However, there will be no elaborate celebrations (so do not plan anything for me because I will not show up) or proclamations. I do not need that and more importantly, I do not want that. Forgive me for any perceived cynicism but I look at turning 50 the very same way I looked at turning 20, 30, and 40 – blessed to be here. I consider myself very pragmatic. Being married for 50 years is an accomplishment worthy of celebration; turning 50 is not. At 50, I will not magically become young again nor will I become suddenly old. It will be what it will be.

For the majority of people, reaching the age of 50 is a very big deal. It is a symbolic number and a banner to be worn proudly on their sleeves. Big parties and gatherings are held in their "honor". Begrudgingly, I've attended a few of these "celebrations" and witnessed the pageantry of it all. They are nice, but what comes after the party is over? Have you suddenly changed for the better? Do you now treat others [any] better? When I retire….that is when I want a party! For me, retirement is an accomplishment, milestone, and turning point, all in one! Reaching 50 is no big deal, but try telling that to most folks. They will promulgate for a national holiday or plan a parade down Main Street.

Living: Reflections

Personally, reaching 50 will bring about more focus on maturation. By age 50, I believe that one should be at a point in their lives where they are still living and planning for tomorrow, but can enjoy the present with a certain degree of "peace of mind". I will focus even more on faith, family, peace, hope, patience, love and charity, wisdom, and good health. Many years ago, a former boss of mine told me "don't sweat the small stuff". Because of the stressful circumstances at the time, I do not think I will ever forget that "elementary" advice. When you really think about it, those words have a profound meaning, and they had a very calming effect on me. I really try to live by her advice every day. Sometimes I am successful, sometimes I am not – but I try. I often find myself giving her advice to others. Therefore, I won't sweat turning 50. I will celebrate another year given to me by the One who gives me everything that I need. However, if you must, go ahead and celebrate turning 50, just do not be content with it. As my Dad used to say, "Moses didn't get his marching orders until he was 80." Living.

Fourteen

Ready

One day, we will all die. That is fact. That is also a promise made by God.

In the sweat of thy face shalt thou eat bread, till thou return unto the ground; for out of it wast thou taken: for dust thou art, and unto dust shalt thou return. **- Genesis 3:19**

Genesis 3:19 is referring to your body returning to the ground from whence it came. Your spirit will live forever – it will be separated from your body at the "physical death" – and will dwell in heaven or hell for all of eternity. Are you ready to die? Are you ready for what comes after your physical death?

Sometimes, I am certain that I am ready to die and go to heaven. At other times, I am not so sure. Being "ready" can be simple or it can be difficult. No one knows the appointed time when they will die. Sure, there may be circumstances or situations (death penalty?) when you "think" you know, but even then, it is not in our control. We cannot control life, and we cannot control death.

Whether I am ready or not depends on my state of mind. There are times when I am so content with knowing that I am going to die that it sends joy through my heart knowing that I will leave this place. It is a feeling of complete peace and confidence that exuberates through mind, body and soul. It is a place where I wish I could be at all times. On other occasions, I fear death. I fail to leave everything up to God. In other words, "self" gets in the way and I began to "think" instead of meditating on things that pleases God.

Being ready requires planning and good decision-making. Again, we know not the appointed time, which is why it is so important to focus on pleasing God at all times. We all will fall short of the mark, but since God forgives, we get extra chances to redeem ourselves. Therefore, it is important that we constantly decide between doing right and doing wrong. It is a maturation process that may take longer for some folks to reach. Nevertheless, we can help each other get there. When we plan, just make sure that God is a part of the planning process. Through daily prayer and the corresponding proper action, you can be ready.

"If you've seen the present, then you've seen everything – as it's ever been since the beginning, as it will be forever".

- *Marcus Aurelius, Roman Emperor*

Living: Reflections

When I first read this quote from the "great Roman philosopher", Marcus Aurelius, I was intrigued. For me it meant living each day as if it were your last. As my mother constantly tells me, "we are living in the last days". Aurelius' quote made a lot of sense to me. However, to really understand that "meditation" by Aurelius, you really need to have some understanding of his thought process, which I found could be rather confusing. He was all about living in the present. Period. There was nothing else. In other words, Aurelius thought that the present is all that you have, so don't worry about planning – for the next life! That is what Aurelius was saying. How wrong! One of the worse things that anyone can do is to be unprepared! Being unprepared speaks volumes about your priorities, planning capabilities, and decision-making. We all need to plan for what is next. Living in the present, for the present, will get you nowhere.

Living: Reflections

In my Father's house are many mansions: if it were not so, I would have told you. I go to prepare a place for you. **- John 14:2**

We have a place prepared for us in Heaven. For those who are faithful to the Lord, Heaven is our inheritance! All we have to do is believe that it is so; decide to go there; plan to go there; make it our number one priority. God is ready for us. Are you prepared? Are you ready? If not, get ready. Heaven is waiting. Living.

Living: Reflections

Fifteen

The Ending...

How far you go in life depends on your being tender with the young, compassionate with the aged, sympathetic with the striving, and tolerant of the weak and the strong -- because someday you will have been all of these.

- *George Washington Carver*

Live long enough and you will become old. This is fact. Living until an old age is truly a blessing from God despite the aches and pains that often accompany old age. Nevertheless, the end of this life will surely come. Have you lived life to the fullest? Have you built a legacy? Have you matured and grown nigh to God? Have you treated your fellow man with love, respect, and kindness? Living is a kaleidoscope of activities that leave indelible impressions that become our very own blueprint. Living can transmit love and hate from the very same spout! We are privileged to have the opportunity to not only exist, but to live. What are you doing to make the very best of this opportunity?

Have you ever noticed the disposition of persons on their deathbeds? They are not reticent. They are at peace with their fate. They display genuine kindness. They are grateful and reflective. They are courageous and focused. They appreciate family and friends. The truth of the matter is that we should all live as if we are dying! Do not wait until you are on your own deathbed to begin living. We were created to live, not to simply exist. We are all special in God's eyes. He wants us to live with fullness and abundance. Because He is the reason we have this opportunity, we should develop a personal relationship with Him.

When the end comes, so will the beginning.

- Marcus H England

At the appointed time, we will all stand before the Throne and be judged individually on how we lived – not how we existed! We cannot depend on our family and friends to put in a good word for us. We will be on our very own and if that does not get your attention, I do not know what will! We will go either to the eternal place of peace or to the eternal fiery furnace with the wailing gnashing of teeth. Were you the very best person that you could be? Did you live to please God? Did you let your light shine so that others could see the Lord through your actions? Did you bring others to the Lord? When my turn comes, I want to hear the words "well done my good and faithful servant….." How about you? We are all a work in progress and none of us are "there" yet. Be persistent. Display courage. Walk by faith. Be encouraged. Be inspired to improve your esteem and be the very best that you can be. Today is a good day to start living!

Nicknames

Pookie, Yogi, Block Head, Chess, Winky, Tight Ike, John Wayne, Flip, Snooky, Beaver, Peter Man, Rooster, Oogie, Scully, Rock, GG, Meat Molly, MD 2020, Big Moe (was the neighborhood bus) Arkie, Crip, Neck Doctor, Tooloo, Birdie, Mutt, Glue, Sambo, Tip, Murdock, Mouse, Fox, Sweet Pea, Godfather, Fat Boy, Dump, Batman, Hully Gully, Ankie, Teedy, Bam Bam, Dr.Spock, Turtle, Gate, Sea Dog, Sugar Doll, Honey, Cap, Plum Pie, Crack, Ray Ray, Houdini, Sweetie, Pee Wee, Snuff, Popeye, Big Joe, and Bugsy.

In my old neighborhood and in many black neighborhoods, nicknames are a staple. Subsequently, they were a part of my early living experience. Nicknames were derived and based on a person's attributes – habits, style, looks, demeanor, etc. They were identifiers and lasted a lifetime (my grandfather called me both Chocolate Chip and [also] Pepper). All of the above played a part in my life- large and small. Some of them were my early role models. I would be hard pressed to say what most of their given names are. Many were my classmates and or relatives and have since passed away. Others were just people in my neighborhood that I personally knew or knew about. Some were of good report – others not so good. Their nicknames remain in my memory if only because they lived. God bless each one of them.

Living: Reflections

Living is not a right. Living is not a science. Living is a God-given privilege. God has given each of us the opportunity to experience life. Are we taking full advantage of this opportunity? Throughout my life, I have experienced a myriad of thoughts, gone through trials, and witnessed things that have influenced how I live my life. Whether you are black, red, brown, Asian, or white, "living" brings about many similarities. Our lives may be different, but living establishes a level of "sameness" – things we all share.

www.ingramcontent.com/pod-product-compliance
Lightning Source LLC
Chambersburg PA
CBHW070545030426
42337CB00016B/2361